ROOD SCREENS

Richard Hayman

SHIRE PUBLICATIONS

Bloomsbury Publishing Plc
PO Box 883, Oxford, OX1 9PL, UK
1385 Broadway, 5th Floor, New York, NY 10018,
USA

E-mail: shire@bloomsbury.com

www.shirebooks.co.uk

SHIRE is a trademark of Osprey Publishing Ltd

First published in Great Britain in 2018

A catalogue record for this book is available from the
British Library.

ISBN: PB 978 1 78442 294 3
        eBook 978 1 78442 295 0
        ePDF 978 1 78442 296 7
        XML 978 1 78442 297 4

18 19 20 21 22   10 9 8 7 6 5 4 3 2 1

Typeset by PDQ Digital Media Solutions, Bungay, UK

Printed in India by Replika Press Private Ltd

Shire Publications supports the Woodland Trust, the
UK's leading woodland conservation charity. Between
2014 and 2018 our donations are being spent on their
Centenary Woods project in the UK.

COVER IMAGE
Front cover: The late fifteenth-century rood screen at
St Stephen's Church, Old Radnor, Powys. Back cover
detail: A roundel from the rood screen at Lapford
(Devon).

TITLE PAGE IMAGE
Rood screens are one of best ways to appreciate the
superb craftsmanship of medieval wood carvers. This
example is from a sixteenth century screen at Lapford.

CONTENTS PAGE IMAGE
West Country rood screens are notable for the intricate
vine trails on the cornice, as in this example at Halse
(Somerset).

AKNOWLEDGEMENTS
All images are by the author except for the front cover
image, courtesy of Alamy.

CONTENTS

THE PRIDE OF THE PARISH   5

ORIGINS AND DEVELOPMENT   9

BUILDING A ROOD SCREEN   15

THE STRUCTURE OF ROOD SCREENS   23

SCREEN DECORATION   29

USE OF SCREENS, LOFTS AND ROODS   39

REFORMATION   45

THE CHURCH OF ENGLAND   53

FURTHER READING   59

PLACES TO VISIT   60

INDEX   64

THE PRIDE OF THE PARISH

THE SMALL CHURCH of Llananno (Powys) in mid-Wales has no village and is an unremarkable building in itself, dating from the 1870s when the medieval church was replaced. It can have enjoyed only a small congregation at the best of times, but the decision to rebuild it seems to have gone beyond the needs of a congregation. The church preserves and protects one of the most magnificent medieval rood screens to survive in England and Wales. It is the best-preserved of a series of screens that were made in mid-Wales in the early sixteenth century, perhaps in a workshop in Newtown (Powys), and is one of a number of notable rood screens to have survived in small, village-less Welsh churches, Partrishow, Llanelieu, Llandefalle (Powys) and Llanegryn (Merioneth) among them.

Surviving rood screens in small churches remind us that they were once considered a necessity, not a luxury. The rood screen was the visual showpiece of the medieval parish church interior, the most important investment made by the parish in enriching the church. It was variously an image gallery and a filter through which the high mass was observed. It stood at the east end of the nave, separating the sacred space of the chancel – where usually only the priests celebrated and where the language of worship was in Latin – from the nave, the secular space of the church frequented by the parishioners.

'Rood' was the Anglo-Saxon word for cross. In the context of the parish church the rood was composed of the

The medieval rood screen at Llananno (Powys) is housed in a small nineteenth-century church. The carved figures date from its restoration in 1880.

crucified Christ flanked by images of the Virgin Mary and John the Evangelist. It was placed high up at the east end of the nave above the rood screen and was accessible from the rood loft. The space behind and above the rood, which in a parish church was usually the chancel arch, was filled with a tympanum, a painted panel usually showing the Last Judgement and known as a Doom painting. The screen and loft were invariably painted and usually gilded, often adorned with images of saints. The whole ensemble therefore epitomised the rich visual culture of medieval Christianity that ended with the Reformation in the mid-sixteenth century. When rood screens were first built they had a dramatic effect which is more difficult to appreciate now, since the nave of the church has acquired so much more furniture in recent centuries.

Although 'rood screen' is the term we now use to describe the ensemble of screen and loft, the term did not gain currency until the nineteenth century, after most of the lofts had been taken down. In the Middle Ages the whole structure was usually known as the rood loft, with some significant regional variations. In Norfolk it was commonly known as a 'perke', in Suffolk a 'candlebeam'. Other variants include 'aler' or allure, derived from a defensive gangway, and solarium (or 'sollar'), which was an upper room in a house.

The rood screen and loft lost their primary function at the time of the Reformation in the mid-sixteenth century. Although screens were not ordered to be removed, many of them have been lost in the subsequent centuries to the vagaries of fashion, the whim of individual parishes and the decay of old woodwork. Nevertheless there is hardly a county in England that cannot boast of some surviving examples. Taken as a whole, the rood screen is part of the rich heritage of our late-medieval parish churches, testament to a golden age of wood carving and of a vibrant popular religion.

The rood screen at Attleborough (Norfolk) extends right across the church and would have dominated the interior before the nave was furnished.

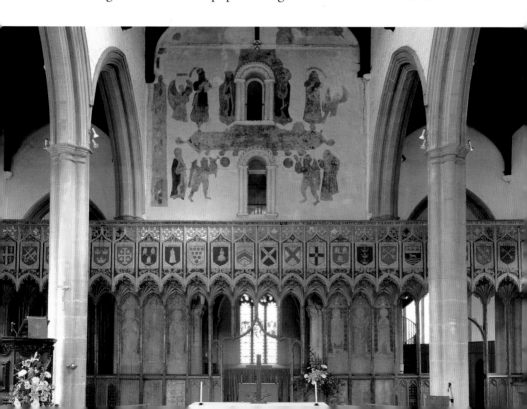

ORIGINS AND DEVELOPMENT

THE EARLIEST SURVIVING rood screens belong to the second half of the thirteenth century – at Stanton Harcourt (Oxfordshire) and Kirkstead (Lincolnshire). There is no evidence that parish churches had rood screens before then, but the concept of a physical and symbolic barrier between the sacred and secular parts of the church was well established in cathedral and monastic churches. Barriers separating these two parts of the church had been in use since ancient times. Colonnade screens are known from Old St Peters in Rome from the sixth century, and several early English churches are known to have had such an arrangement, including Rochester Cathedral, Canterbury St Pancras (Kent), Brixworth (Northamptonshire), Bradwell-on-sea (Essex) and Repton (Derbyshire). At Reculver (Kent) the arrangement survived until the early nineteenth century, in the form of a three-bay arcade between the nave and chancel. However, these were monastic foundations and the scheme was not adopted for smaller churches. In smaller surviving Anglo-Saxon churches, such as Escomb (Durham) and Bradford-on-Avon (Wiltshire), the opening from nave to chancel is a narrow arch, and a screen was hardly necessary since the boundary between nave and chancel was already visually decisive.

Another type of division between nave and chancel was the pulpitum (Latin for stage or platform), found in cathedrals and monasteries. Monks, canons, nuns and friars followed a daily series of prayer and acts of worship, but they were

OPPOSITE
The late-fourteenth century stone screen at Great Bardfield (Essex) fills the chancel arch and is a type that pre-dates the later screens with lofts. The figure of Christ was added in 1896.

The thirteenth-century screen at Stanton Harcourt (Oxfordshire) is one of the earliest surviving rood screens.

not intended to be performed in public. A pulpitum closed off the west end of the chancel, giving privacy for these self-contained acts of worship. Therefore the pulpitum is not a direct forerunner of the rood screen. In rare cases did the pulpitum act effectively as a rood screen, but in such churches, like Crediton and Ottery St Mary (Devon), the churches were shared between a parish and a religious house.

In Norman churches the division between nave and chancel was emphasised by means of decorated chancel arches, usually the most richly decorated feature of the interior of a Norman church. Decoration of chancel arches was concentrated on the west face, making the chancel arch, and view into the chancel, the focal point of the interior. It was, perhaps, enough to make the chancel arch a symbolic if not physical barrier between the two. From the twelfth century the chancel arch became wider, giving a better view into the chancel, and was flanked by blank walls where side altars were set up, an arrangement still visible at Barfreston (Kent). Gothic chancel arches, from c.1200, are plainer in decoration, but are likely to span the entire width of the chancel and are therefore usually wider than twelfth-century arches. This trend continued throughout the Middle Ages, to the extent that in many churches there is no chancel arch at all, a feature especially associated with Devon. The rood screen therefore developed to mark the transition point between nave and chancel.

By the fourteenth century rood screens were evidently widespread in parish churches. There are documentary references to several of them in London parish churches, including St Dion's (1342), St Benet Gracechurch Street (1342), St Martin Vintry (1350) and St Christopher le Stocks (1352). Enlargement of chancel arches in the fourteenth century can sometimes be linked directly with the erection of

The rood screen at Dunster (Somerset) spans the nave and aisles and separates the parish church from the east end, which was a small Benedictine priory.

a rood screen, as at Rivenhall (Essex) *c.*1325, Hales (Norfolk) and West Harnham (Wiltshire). Not all of these early rood screens were in grand urban churches. Pixley (Herefordshire) is a small rural church but it had a rood screen by the fourteenth century, part of which has survived.

Most surviving rood screens belong to the fifteenth and sixteenth centuries, but we know from documentary sources

The stone rood screen at Welsh Newton (Herefordshire) was built in the fourteenth century, an example of how stone screens have an architectural character.

that many of them must be second-generation screens. For example, churchwardens' accounts for various Somerset parishes mention the replacement of old rood screens – Glastonbury St John the Baptist in 1439, Tintinhull in 1451–2 and Yatton in 1455. It appears that there was a fashion for enriched screens at this time, a period in which many parish churches were rebuilt in the Perpendicular style and often furnished with seating for the first time. So the rood screen as we know it best comes from a golden age of lay spirituality and prosperity that continued to flourish until the time of the Reformation.

Screens were also erected around side chapels in parish churches, the prevalence of which increased throughout the Middle Ages, as individuals built their own chantry chapels where prayers could be said for them in perpetuity, or groups of people formed guilds, which had their own chapels. These 'parclose screens' gave some privacy to these chapels, usually when they were set up in the nave aisles. Often rood and parclose screens were built as a single integral structure. Where they stand alone, parclose screens differ from rood screens because they do not need a loft, but otherwise they are of similar appearance.

Roods have an earlier, independent origin. These crosses were set up in Anglo-Saxon churches and fragments of them have survived, including painted figures at Headbourne Worthy (Hampshire) and Bradford-on-Avon (Wiltshire). A decree issued by Archbishop Lanfranc of Canterbury (1070–1089) was for a large rood or crucifix to be placed over the entrance to the choir in monastic churches. Their prevalence at this time in parish churches and private chapels is unknown, however. Several twelfth-century churches in Sussex (including Coombs and Clayton) have paintings of Christ on the east

One of the earliest surviving Norfolk rood screens is at Edingthorpe, which has tracery in fourteenth-century style. The painted figures were added later.

St Margarets (Herefordshire) is a small church with a narrow chancel arch and did not need a screen. It has a loft supported on posts (known as the veranda type) and this was accessed from the chancel.

wall of the nave, perhaps forerunners of the formal rood group. However, a rood was not compulsory in parish churches – it is not mentioned in the Exeter statutes of 1287, which list items necessary to ornament the parish church – although they probably existed in churches by this time and became more frequent in the centuries that followed.

Parclose screens, like this example from Barking (Suffolk), are similar in form to rood screens, but have no coving or loft.

BUILDING A ROOD SCREEN

IN A PARISH church the chancel was the responsibility of the rector (sometimes the clergyman of the parish, but more often the abbot of a monastery or the lord of the manor), while the remainder of the church was the responsibility of the parish. This division had been regulated by the Fourth Lateran Council of 1215. It meant that the rood screen would be the responsibility of the parish, and necessitated the emergence of the churchwarden to administer funds and organise building and other works. It also gave an incentive for the parish to invest in beautifying its own church.

Churchwardens organised the raising of funds for the building of rood screens. In theory the whole parish could contribute, as funds were raised by various means: church ales, money collected for candles, individual donations or bequests, the hiring of tapers and processional crosses for funerals, and by burial fees. For benefactors, large or small, a gift was a spiritual investment and sometimes it was made explicit that they wanted the prayers of the living after they had died. For example, John Mottes of Thorpe by Haddiscoe (Norfolk) gave money for a new screen in 1534 on the condition that a memorial mass was said for him once a year after his death. On the screen at Trunch (Norfolk), completed in 1502, an inscription asks the parish to pray for the souls of all of the benefactors.

People paid varying amounts, often to a general screen fund but occasionally for a specific part of it. When a new rood

OPPOSITE
Nymet Tracey (Devon) rood screen is brightly painted on the west face, but the east face was never painted, a graphic demonstration of how the screen was funded by and for the parish rather than the priests.

The parish commissioned the woodwork and the painting of a screen separately, like this example at Bovey Tracey (Devon).

screen was built at Glastonbury St John in 1439, individual donations ranged from one pound to one penny. Parish guilds also donated significant sums to screens and other church building projects. Two panels from the rood screen at Ipswich St Matthew (Suffolk) depict nine men and seven women, probably the brethren and sisters of the Erasmus

The screen at Kentisbeare (Devon) was funded largely by John Whiting in the 1530s. The gold effect was made by silver leaf with a yellow glaze.

guild that contributed money for the screen. Several craft and religious guilds gave money for the rebuilding of Bodmin church (Cornwall) between 1469 and 1472, including for its screen. The churchwardens made a list of 447 donors in total, about seventy of whom were women, showing how the funding of church-building projects, including screens, was a collective effort.

Sometimes the screen was paid for by a single patron, examples of which are John and Agnes Albrede at Woodbridge (Suffolk), Joan Tackle at Honiton (Devon), and John and Benedicta Alblastyr at Worstead (Norfolk). This was rare, however, because the painting and decoration of a rood screen was a long-term project and money was given at different stages of completion. Painting and gilding was often paid for separately. Richard Clemens, a Norwich tanner, gave the considerable sum of £10 in 1534 to be used for gilding of the rood loft in his parish church, whenever the work was to be undertaken. At Southwold (Suffolk), £20 was given toward the new screen in 1459, but money for painting the Doom was given in 1474 and another bequest in 1481 was for painting the rood beam.

Occasionally the names of donors appear on the screens themselves. In the 1530s the screen at North Burlingham (Norfolk) was substantially funded by two patrons, Thomas Bennet and his family for the north side of the screen, John and Cecily Blake (whose names appear with the portrayals of their

Thomas Wymer had an inscription recording his gift to the rood screen at Aylsham (Norfolk) in 1509, with paintings that included a portrait of himself next to his namesake saint.

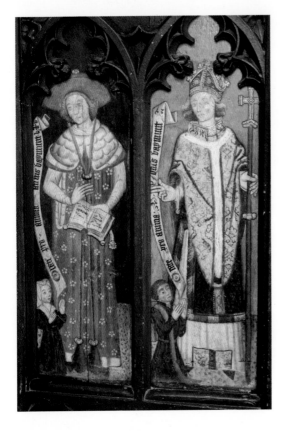

At Foxley (Norfolk) the screen doors depict St Ambrose and St Jerome, together with images of John Baymont and his wife, who gave 5 marks for painting the screen.

patron saints John the Baptist and Cecilia) for the south side. Foxley has the praying figures of John Baymont and his wife, although they gave only 5 marks (£3/8/4) for painting the screen, perhaps a deathbed addition following larger benefactions for building the screen.

As the rood screen became the focus of the interior, there was incentive to ensure that it was the most magnificent object possessed by the parish. Several contracts exist for the building of rood screens. Many stipulate that a screen must equal or surpass a neighbouring work. At Morebath (Devon), for example, the wood carver William Popyll was asked in 1535 to make a screen similar to the one at neighbouring Brushford (Somerset). The churchwardens of Yatton sent three men to Easton-in-Gordano (also Somerset) to see the screen there. A new rood screen at Hackington (Kent), on the outskirts of Canterbury, was commissioned in 1519 from Michael Bonversall of Hythe, who was required to make a copy of the screen at Canterbury Holy Cross (part of the screen survives, re-sited in the south transept). John Nun and Roger Bell, both Suffolk carpenters, were contracted to build the rood screen at St Mary the Great in Cambridge. The specification stipulates that the western side should follow the example of Triplow (Cambridgeshire), the eastern side Gazeley (Suffolk).

There was more than mere rivalry in these clauses. In some cases design drawings must have been produced – for example at Banwell (Somerset), where the carpenter was paid 4d 'for papers to draw the draft of the rodeloft'. But for the most part there do not seem to have been preliminary drawings and the identification of exemplars for the carvers to follow was a means of drawing up an informal agreement between churchwardens and carvers. Perhaps in some cases the exemplars were previous works by the same craftsmen. Occasionally exemplars were sought from far afield, presumably on the advice either of craftsmen or priests. At Eton College (Buckinghamshire), the contract for building a rood screen in 1475 named Winchester College and St Thomas of Acre in London as examples to work to.

A detailed specification has survived for the rood screen built at Stratton (Cornwall) in 1534–39. (Unfortunately the screen does not survive. The present screen in the church was built in

When complete, this screen at Brushford (Somerset) was the model for the rood screen at neighbouring Morebath (Devon).

Atherington has the only rood screen in Devon that retains its loft parapet. John Pares worked on carving the screen in the 1540s and was also employed on making the screen at Stratton in Cornwall.

1901 by the architect E.H. Sedding.) It was built by John Daw of Lawhitton and John Pares, a carpenter, carver and joiner who lived at Northlew (Devon) and who later worked on the rood screen at Atherington (Devon). For the contract at Stratton, the rood screen at St Kew, parclose screens at St Columb Major and windows at Week St Mary (presumably referring to images of saints) are all cited as exemplars. The craftsmen were to be paid by the foot and the specification included the position of the screen, its height, the associated altars and images, plus necessary alterations to the walls that included a stair and a window in the south wall. The screen and loft cost £82/11/4. There are other contracts that specify a price per foot for the screen and loft. For example Michael Bonversall was paid 20 shillings per foot for the screen at Hackington (Kent) in a contract that gave him four years to complete the work.

Rood screens were probably prefabricated in workshops, and then erected on site ready for painting and gilding. The images, where carved or painted, were not necessarily the work of the carvers who built the screens. Three men were responsible for the new rood loft built at Morebath (Devon): William Popyll, the carver, John Painter and John Creche, the gilder. At Yatton, John Crosse was the carver but appears not to have been the 'image maker' responsible for the sixty-nine images on the screen. At Stratton, Daw and Pares carved the rood, but beautification continued after the rood screen structure was complete.

The screen at Chawleigh (Devon) spans the width of the church. Often the cost of a screen was calculated by a price per foot.

THE STRUCTURE OF ROOD SCREENS

ALTHOUGH MOST ROOD screens are built of wood, a minority of screens were constructed in stone, which includes many of the surviving early rood screens. There are no surviving stone rood lofts, however, but the fourteenth-century screens at Stebbing and Great Bardfield (both Essex) fill the chancel arch. Stone screens are part of the architecture of a church and have a different character to wooden screens.

The vast majority of rood screens and lofts were of wood. In earlier medieval churches the woodwork is usually modest but in the fifteenth and sixteenth centuries the art of wood carving flourished, which is observed not just in screens and lofts, but in bench ends, pulpits and especially church roofs. The main advantages of wood over stone were that it was cheaper and offered more opportunity for intricate decoration. For this reason the simpler forms of rood screen look to be early in style, although this can be misleading. Few surviving rood screens are precisely dated and so simplicity is not necessarily synonymous with an early date. The richness of screen work varied according to the available funds for building them.

The construction of rood screens and lofts was based on the techniques of timber-framed construction, combined with decoration that borrowed the language of stone carving. The lowest element of a wooden screen is the sill, a strong timber beam at floor level. Set into the sill are the vertical standards, or posts, that support the loft. The solid lower section of the

OPPOSITE
Rood screens often showcase the skills of the medieval carpenter with their intricate tracery, of which the rood screen at Partrishow (Powys) is a fine example.

A late-medieval stone screen at Broughton (Oxfordshire).

screen is referred to in some contemporary documents as the wainscot, but is usually now called the dado and rises to waist height. Above dado level is open tracery, in square-headed or arched bays, with a wider central bay incorporating the doors to the chancel. In the earlier wooden screens the uprights, or muntins, are rounded in imitation of stone shafts, a style to which carvers returned in the mid-sixteenth century when they adopted Renaissance style, but in most cases the muntins are similar to the chamfered stone mullions found in contemporary windows. The tracery likewise follows the prevailing architectural style of the time, and in most surviving rood screens is an ornate form of Perpendicular.

The loft is supported by coving which projects on either side of the screen to the bressumer, the beam that supports the cornice and loft front. The underside of the coving is decorated with blind panels defined by moulded ribs, or else is an imitation in wood of stone vaulting. Sometimes

The tracery on rood screens is based on contemporary window tracery, as in this fine example from Berry Pomeroy (Devon).

the coving projects so far that an additional veranda of posts is needed to support it. Screens of this type can be seen in many churches near the English–Welsh border, such as Llanelieu (Powys), Burghill and St Margarets (Herefordshire).

The floor of the rood loft is concealed behind a cornice, generally made up of bands of foliage, and an upper band of cresting, also known as brattishing. In some screens there is a loft front, or parapet, that incorporates an image gallery, adorned with either painted or sculpted figures. The rood was fixed to the rood loft or onto a separate beam, sometimes positioned well above the loft and fixed to the walls.

Carving of screens differed according to region, although there are some general similarities. Lofty East Anglian churches have correspondingly lofty rood screens with arched bays. Only a minority of East Anglian screens had central doors, and the survival of original rood lofts is comparatively poor. The churches of western England and Wales are smaller and the rood screens are therefore lower. A happy consequence of this is that the loft coving and cornices are often more richly detailed. Many of the south-west screens also span the nave and the aisles, giving the screen a pronounced horizontal emphasis. The coving of the rood loft is also very much region-based. In Wales and the Marches it comprises moulded ribs with leaf bosses at the intersections, and panels originally intended be be painted. West Country screens of the sixteenth century have coving closely modelled on fan vaulting, incorporating cusped or other decorative panels, of which there are numerous fine examples across Somerset, Devon and Cornwall. In south-west England and in the Marches of Wales the cornices above the coving are usually decorated with vine trails, although there is considerable inventiveness in this basic motif. In many of the mid-Wales screens, including

The veranda-type rood loft at Llanelieu (Powys) is very deep. It retains its tympanum with stencilled decoration and the shadow of the rood.

The coving on the rood screen at Aymestrey (Herefordshire) imitates Gothic vaulting and is typical of screens in the Marches.

Although the loft has been taken down, the rood-loft stairway, lit by a small window, has survived in the north wall at Llandefalle (Powys).

The medieval rood screen, loft and tympanum at Bettws Newydd (Monmouthshire) form the most complete surviving rood group in England or Wales. Only the rood image itself and the original paint have been removed.

Llandefalle, Llananno and Pennant Melangell, the vine trails spew from the mouths of wyverns, a variation on the popular green-man motif. The majority of surviving loft fronts are in the England–Wales border region. Many once had images painted or carved on them, but the survival rate of these images is poor. The finest painted loft front is on the screen at Attleborough (Norfolk), but its depictions of the arms of the English and Welsh dioceses date from the early seventeenth century.

Early roods were fixed to a beam that was built into the chancel arch. Evidence of such early rood beams is apparent in numerous churches – Old Shoreham (Sussex) has a twelfth-century beam and Binstead (Sussex) has the sawn-off stumps of a finely moulded beam of c.1260. After the widespread introduction of rood lofts the rood could also be fixed to the loft parapet, but were generally fixed to the tops of rood beams, in order to give them a more lofty presence. Occasionally the rood was suspended from the beam. At Cullompton (Devon) the foot of the Rood rested on the rood loft and was set into sockets of a carved sill

The former tympanum at Wenhaston (Suffolk) portrays the Day of Judgement. The shadow of the rood figures is clearly visible. At the bottom are texts painted over the original work during the Reformation.

known as a Golgotha, replicating the scene of Calvary where Christ was crucified.

The rood loft was reached by ladder or stair. Mural stairs, the winding stairs which are often housed inside a polygonal turret projecting on the north side of the nave, a sight common in Somerset, were known as a vyse or vice. Behind and above the rood was a tympanum, ideally filling the space under the chancel arch. The best example of a Doom is from Wenhaston (Suffolk), rediscovered in 1892 under layers of whitewash during restoration work, although it is no longer in its original position under the chancel arch. Partial survivals are also at Patcham (Sussex), Coventry Holy Trinity and Salisbury St Thomas (Wiltshire). Above the rood loft the nave roof was enriched, known as a ceilure or ceiling (also now as a canopy of honour). To light the rood there was often a window at eaves height in the south wall of the nave, which is easily distinguished because it is set higher than the other nave windows and is at the east end.

The roof directly above the rood screen was often enriched, like this fine example at Kings Nympton (Devon).

SCREEN DECORATION

Painting and gilding of the rood screen began as soon as it was set up, even if it was a protracted project that could last for several years. The show side of the rood screen was the west side and the painting was sometimes confined to this side. The first coating was intended to seal the grain and create a smooth surface. It was usually of lead white or gesso. A primer, usually iron oxide reds and ochres, was then applied, and it was on this surface that the oil-based paints and the gilding, using gold or silver leaf, was applied. Reds, blues, greens, black and white were the main colours used on screens. Blue was obtained from woad, greens were copper based and red was derived from vermillion. Paint on a screen took several weeks to apply, and months to dry. Only afterwards could it be glazed, which means applying a translucent colour over the opaque paint to give it more richness and depth. Although gilded surfaces could not be painted, glazing could be applied – at Kentisbeare (Devon) silver leaf with a yellow glaze gave the appearance of gold. The glaze took as long to dry as the paint, after which it was varnished using copal, a hard resin derived from tropical trees.

Many surviving rood screens retain supporting images of saints, although the distribution of these survivals is very uneven. The vast majority are in Norfolk (eighty surviving screens with some or all of their images), Suffolk (thirty-nine) and Devon (forty-two). Most of these images are painted on the dado of the screen. They reflect an important trend

OPPOSITE
Images of the Evangelists Luke and Matthew are on the screen at Torbryan (Devon).

On the screen
at Cawston
(Norfolk)
St Matthew is
depicted in a
contemporary
style with bald
head and glasses.

in medieval Christianity – the late-medieval devotion to saints based on images, superseding the early-medieval devotion that had been based on relics. Non-representational imagery and inscriptions are also found painted onto rood screens. However, not all screens were designed to have an image gallery on the dado or the loft front. Some dado panels have relief carving, such as the Renaissance-style decoration at Marwood (Devon), passion symbols at St Levan (Cornwall), foliage trails or linenfold panelling. Some of the finest surviving loft fronts have pierced tracery panels.

Non-representational painted imagery is the most difficult to date precisely, because most such imagery could post-date the Reformation. Some Devon screens, such as South Pool, have Renaissance-style painted decoration which could plausibly date from before the Reformation because these motifs are also used in the screen carving, and at Blackawton it is clearly so because it incorporates monograms of Katherine of Aragon and Henry VIII. Stencilled patterns of fleur-de-lys, floral or plainer geometric or diaper patterns are also found, for example at Thompson (Norfolk), while Willingham (Cambridgeshire) is decorated with popinjays. Monograms such as the familiar IHS (the first three letters of the Greek spelling of Jesus) were another form of stencilled decoration.

The adornment of the screen with images was clearly the ambition of most parishes, and was perhaps sometimes a

Saints Stephen, Sitha, Peter the Martyr and St Margaret of Antioch are on the dado of the screen at Hennock (Devon).

At Acle (Norfolk) the screen dado is painted with stencilled monograms. The E with crossed arrows represents St Edmund, a popular East Anglian saint.

reason for replacing an earlier rood screen. The painting of screen images was a major expense and was carefully planned before the work was undertaken. The contract for making the rood screen at Stratton (Cornwall), for example, is very specific about the images that were to adorn it. The images for the side altars, to be of Saint Armel (a cult encouraged by Henry VII after he was saved from shipwreck off the French coast) and the Blessed Virgin Mary, reflected their dedications.

The iconography of the screen was not random. The figures represented were those who would accompany Christ when he came to judge the living and their presence spoke to the congregation of the role of saints as intercessors with Christ in the here and now, but also on the last day. The screen images were set below the rood

The rood screen at Horsham St Faith (Norfolk), dated 1528, hosts an eclectic mix of saints, including St Catherine of Siena, seen here holding a heart. The figure was defaced during the Reformation.

and the doom painting and the whole ensemble was a visual representation of the Christian universe, the filter through which the Mass was observed.

The choice of figures for the dado or loft was carefully planned. Alice Chester funded a new screen at Bristol All Saints in 1483, on account of the pre-existing screen being overly plain. She consulted 'the worshipful of the parish' to decide on the iconography of the twenty-two screen images, but there is no evidence that she sought the counsel of the priest. However, screens rarely had single benefactors and in most churches the choice must have been a collective investment by the parish. The saints upon it reflected the preferences of the congregation and therefore give an intimate insight into the religious lives of lay worshippers.

In some places there are obscure saints that suggest a well-read and sophisticated lay patron. It would account for the appearance of, for example, Saints Alexis and Catherine of Siena at Torbryan (Devon). Likewise, the appearance of Catherine of Siena and St Bridget of Sweden on the screen at Horsham St Faith (Norfolk), dated 1528, was probably at the behest of the screen's principal donor, William Wulcy, who had probably read the devotional writings of both women. Curiously, the patron saints of churches were not especially favoured when it came to decorating the screen, probably because an image of the patron saint was usually in the chancel.

There were mainstream saints portrayed on rood screens across the country, and also local saints with a limited geographical reach. It was common for the rood screen doors to be painted with the Four Doctors of the Latin Church – Gregory, Ambrose, Augustine and Jerome – the men whose teaching provided the framework of medieval Christian worship. The Four Evangelists were sometimes treated in a similar way, and were identifiable by their signs: an angel for Matthew, winged lion for Mark, winged ox for Luke and eagle for John. The Twelve Apostles are the most common saints to appear on screens, often bearing scrolls on which the Apostles' Creed was inscribed. The apostles were important because they were the primary witnesses of the life, death and resurrection of Christ. Other Biblical saints like the Virgin Mary and St Mary Magdalene had a similar

Saints Matthew and Mark on the rood screen at Bramfield (Suffolk).

On the dado at Chudleigh (Devon) are alternate apostles and prophets. On this panel are Philip, Malachi, Bartholomew and Joel.

The north end of the screen at Barton Turf (Norfolk) shows part of the sequence showing the orders of angels, with Saints Apollonia and Sitha to the left.

St George slays the dragon, on the rood screen at Ranworth (Norfolk).

importance. Old Testament prophets appear on some screens and where they are grouped with apostles they articulate the medieval belief in Old Testament prophecy and New Testament fulfilment, a scheme well demonstrated at Chudleigh, Bovey Tracey and Kenton (all Devon). Barton Turf (Norfolk) and Southwold (Suffolk) are the best surviving of several screens that illustrated the heavenly hierarchy, in the form of nine orders of angels.

Mostly, images of saints can be identified by their attributes. Some of these remain commonly known, such as the dragon for George, wheel for Catherine or saltire cross for Andrew, but others have lapsed into obscurity since the Reformation, reminding us of the loss of our visual culture. So Lawrence is shown with a gridiron, Stephen with a bunch of rocks, John the apostle with a poisoned chalice, Barbara with a tower.

FAR LEFT
The popular Devon saint Sidwell can be identified at Whimple as a woman carrying her own head, referencing her martyrdom.

LEFT
A man holding a large boot at Hennock (Devon) can be identified as Sir John Schorne who, despite never being canonised, was a cult figure in parts of England.

Rarely are they identified by name, but there are exceptions on Devon screens at Ipplepen and Wolborough.

Many non-Biblical saints enjoyed a national or local cult. English kings are one example of the former, most often Edward the Confessor, canonised in 1161. Popular Devon saints found on rood screens include Sidwell, whose cult at Exeter was established before AD 1000, and Urith, who had a shrine at Chittlehampton. Popular East Anglian saints are often encountered on rood screens: Edmund was the martyred ninth-century king of East Anglia, Etheldreda was founding abbess of Ely and her sister Withburga lived as a solitary in Norfolk. Another reason for regional preferences was the influence of the church itself. In 1337 Bishop Grandison of Exeter issued an Ordinal in which numerous saints were commemorated, and which also feature widely on rood screens in the diocese, such as Margaret, Lawrence, John the Baptist and Stephen.

The intercessory importance of saints is well represented by the fashion for helper saints. St Apollonia was invoked in prayers by toothache sufferers, St Margaret of Antioch was

protector of women in childbirth. Sir John Schorne was not a saint, but his cult became popular in East Anglia and elsewhere. He had been rector of North Marston in Buckinghamshire until his death in 1313, and was famed for forcing the devil into a boot and for striking his staff on the ground where a well sprang forth. He was invoked in prayers by sufferers of gout (i.e. the devil in a boot). He appears on Norfolk rood screens at Cawston, Gateley and Suffield, and at Alphington, Hennock and Wolborough in Devon.

Many of the female saints already mentioned were virgin martyrs and sometimes they were grouped on rood screens, usually opposite the place where the women of the parish stood or sat during the mass. They also document a strong female involvement in deciding the iconography of the rood screen. At North Elmham (Norfolk) virgin martyrs occupy the whole south side of the screen, while at Westhall (Suffolk) and Litcham (Norfolk) there are eight virgin martyrs on the south and north sides of the screen respectively.

Images on rood screens were derived from their representation in statue niches and stained-glass panels. Toward the end of the Middle Ages the influence of book illustrations found its way on to rood screens. These depict narrative scenes rather than simple figures. At Ashton (Devon) this was achieved by means of scrolls with inscriptions related to the Annunciation and Visitation. Scenes in the life of the Virgin Mary – Annunciation, Nativity and Coronation – are shown elsewhere on Devon screens at Torbryan, Plymtree and Hennock. In Norfolk there are similar narrative scenes at Loddon.

The Adoration of the Magi at Loddon (Norfolk) is an example of the late-medieval fashion for narrative scenes on rood screens.

Paintings on the east side of the screen at Ashton (Devon) portray the Annunciation and demi-figures of prophets with scrolls.

USE OF SCREENS, LOFTS AND ROODS

THE ROOD SCREEN had practical and liturgical functions. The rood loft emerged because a convenient way was needed of gaining access to the rood. Candles, lamps, tapers and torches were set up on the rood beam in order to light or honour the rood. The rood beam at Westwell (Kent) was said to be large enough to accommodate sixty candlesticks. The number of lights on the rood beam varied throughout the year, being especially important at patronal festivals. The provision of candle wax was the largest ongoing cost of maintaining the rood loft. The churchwardens' accounts for Exeter St Petroc reveal the importance of lights on the loft: 22lb of wax was bought in 1477–8 at the festival of St Petroc; 72lb of candle wax were purchased in 1512–13 at a cost of 3 shillings, while in 1541–42 100lb of candles were lit before the rood.

Churchwardens' accounts also make regular references to pageants on the rood loft. These were tapestries, paintings or tableaux representing religious scenes or allegorical devices and seem to have been common in the West Country. Thomas Martin, rector of Norton Fitzwarren (Somerset) left money in 1509 for a pageant to be painted on the rood loft at Pilton (Somerset). A new pageant was carved for Exeter St Petroc in 1482–3, on a rood loft that had been completed in 1459, showing that they were not an integral feature of the original construction.

Occasionally the figure of Christ was clothed, information that has usually been passed down because such roods were a target for iconoclasts at the Reformation. The best-known example is from Chilham (Kent), where in 1543 Christ was clothed in a green satin coat and wore silver shoes. Other costly embellishments to roods included jewels, gilt crosses and a crown. The Chilham and some other roods attracted pilgrims. The 'Cross of Ludlow' (Shropshire) was reputed to save people from damnation, while the rood at Malmesbury Abbey (Wiltshire) apparently cured a girl with curvature of the spine, a paralysed woman and a blind fisherman.

The loft was generally used by singers. The use of Sarum, the form of Christian liturgy most commonly used in England in the fourteenth, fifteenth and early sixteenth centuries, mentions the presence of singers on the pulpitum, which would translate to the rood loft in a parish church. It explains why organs were set up in rood lofts, as recorded at Louth (Lincolnshire) in 1500 and again in 1508–9. Churchwardens' accounts often refer to organs in the plural when they were taken down in the 1550s. Use of the loft for singers continued after the Reformation. The medieval organ in the rood loft at Honiton St Michael (Devon) was still in use in 1829 (the church was destroyed by fire in 1911).

Some lofts were capacious enough to accommodate an altar before the rood, such as at Grantham (Lincolnshire). The rood loft was also occasionally a convenient place to store parish documents and books in a wooden chest. Bristol St Ewens had a clock on the rood loft by 1521.

During Mass at the high altar on a Sunday the screen acted partly as a barrier, but it also framed a view of proceedings in the chancel. At the critical moment of the Mass a bell was rung to warn worshippers of the Elevation of the Host, the moment when the bread and wine became the body and blood of Christ. The bell warned worshippers who were kneeling in private prayer to look to the east, although if they were kneeling close to the screen their view would

Holes known as squints were cut into the dado of rood screens so that kneeling members of the congregation could witness the Elevation of the Host at Mass. This example is from Church Hanborough (Oxfordshire).

be blocked. The solution was to cut small holes, known as squints, in the dado of the screen so that kneeling members of the congregation could gain a view into the chancel. The rood screen usually has a door between nave and chancel, although they are generally absent on East Anglian rood screens, where there is an arched opening instead. The priest passed through the door to read the epistle and gospel at Mass on Sundays, to carry sacred objects such as the pax brede (a small ivory tablet with the image of the rood that was kissed by the congregation at the parish Mass) and the consecrated host on Easter Sunday, the day of the year when the laity took communion.

The Use of Sarum provided for processions to the rood on special occasions – after vespers on Saturdays between Easter Sunday and Advent, and at Mass on Easter Sunday when Psalm 113 was sung before it. But the most important annual ritual concerning the rood was the procession on Palm Sunday. During Lent the rood was veiled, a long-established practice that is recorded from the time of King Alfred in the ninth century. On Palm Sunday, when the procession had reached its final station in front of the rood screen, the veil was lifted,

The image of Pity at Wellingham (Norfolk), where Christ is surrounded by images from his Passion, was originally a reredos behind an altar set up against the rood screen.

The rood screen at Ranworth retains its original painted decoration, including the saints behind the restored nave altars.

at which the parish knelt before it and sang the anthem *Ave Rex Noster* (Hail our king). Mass was then begun and, during the reading of the Gospels, parishioners made crosses with sticks and string. To add dramatic effect the Gospel was often sung from the rood loft. Writing in the late-sixteenth century about the form of worship before the Reformation, Roger Martyn of Long Melford (Suffolk) remembered that, when

he was a boy, the priest would sing the Passion (chapters 18 and 19 from John's Gospel) from the loft on Good Friday, standing by the rood.

Although the screen seems to mystify the performance of the Mass in a sacred space closed off to lay people, in practice many simple masses were said during the weekdays (known as low masses), not in the chancel but in the nave. Their presence gives credence to contemporary accounts that people often crowded round the altar, sometimes even chatting with each other, while the priest was reciting the liturgy. Where altars were set up against the screen, the screen became the backdrop, or reredos, to the ceremony rather than a visual filter, or barrier. Nave altars were once commonplace and their former presence is often easy to identify by a blank area on the rood screen dado. Ranworth (Norfolk) is the best surviving example of this arrangement because it retains its images of saints behind the side altars. At Ranworth the altars are replacements, however, but at Partrishow (Powys) the original stone altars have survived in their original positions, identifiable by the five consecration crosses carved on them. These nave altars were controlled and often owned by the laity, either as individuals, families or parish guilds. The laity decided what masses would be said at the nave altars, whether requiem masses, or masses said in honour of the Virgin Mary or other favoured saints, and were an important part of late-medieval Christian worship.

At Partrishow (Powys) the medieval stone altars set against the rood screen have survived in place.

REFORMATION

THE REFORMATION OF the mid-sixteenth century saw a radical shift in forms of worship and in the physical appearance of the church, which also affected the appearance, function and existence of rood screens and lofts. A new form of worship was introduced that emphasised scripture, rejecting much of traditional Christian practice for which there was no Biblical authority. The Mass was replaced by Holy Communion, while English and Welsh replaced Latin as the language of worship. The interior of the parish church was transformed: images of saints on the walls, windows and screens were removed and in many cases replaced by Biblical texts. However, the Reformation was not a single event but a long process of change. Even after the king was declared head of the Church of England in 1534, and after the first monasteries were dissolved in 1536, there were new rood screens in parish churches. Brenchley (Kent) is dated 1536, Cranbrook (Kent) 1543 and Bletchingley (Surrey) 1546.

Many rood screens were adorned with images but it was usually the rood itself that became a target for reformers. Radicals disapproved of images that encouraged idolatry – images were the work of men but were sometimes worshipped as if they were manifestations of God. They attracted pilgrims who knelt, prayed and lit candles before them, or censed them with incense. There were well-documented, if isolated, attacks on rood screens and roods before such images had been formally proscribed. Some parishioners of Rickmansworth

OPPOSITE
Blackawton (Devon) rood screen has Renaissance decoration and the initials of Henry VIII and Katherine of Aragon, an ironic show of loyalty to the crown on the eve of the Reformation.

The figure of St Benedict on the screen at North Burlingham was probably defaced less than twenty years after it was painted.

(Hertfordshire) were responsible for burning images in the parish church in 1522, with the rood their main target, but the fire got out of hand and burned the rood loft. In 1532 three men were hanged for taking down the rood at Dovercourt (Essex), according to John Foxe who later in the century hailed them as Protestant martyrs. The rood had come to the attention of radicals because it was clothed in a coat, which was burned by a fourth accomplice.

A Royal Injunction of 1536 criticised the cult of images, but it was a second Injunction, issued in 1538, that ordered images to be removed from churches. This was targeted at images that attracted pilgrims and offerings, described as the 'detestable offence of idolatry', but few rood screen images probably fell under that category, while the screens and lofts themselves were not implicated. The Injunction specifically stated that candles were to be banned, exceptions including 'the light that commonly goes across the church by the rood loft', and a light before the sacrament on the altar.

The Injunction of 1538 gave encouragement to Protestants who loathed certain notorious roods. Boxley (Kent) had been a place of pilgrimage on the road to Canterbury. Its rood was known as the Rood of Grace and supposedly had miraculous powers. The figure of Christ could turn its eyes and move its lower lip in response to the entreaties of ailing supplicants.

Henry VIII donated half a mark (6s 8d) to it after his accession and the papal legate Lorenzo Campeggio visited it in 1518. In fact it was just a simple puppet with priests pulling the strings, the exposure of which was a propaganda coup for the reformers. In 1538 the image was taken down and brought to St Paul's Cross in London where, before a large crowd, Bishop Hilsey of Rochester preached against the blasphemous deception of images, showing the congregation how it worked by pulling on the strings himself. The image was broken into small pieces when it was thrown to the congregation. Another example

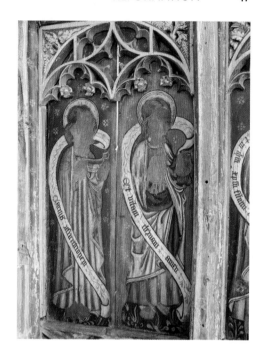

Defaced apostles on the screen at Ringland (Norfolk), with scrolls of the Apostles' Creed.

in the same year was the rood from St Margaret Pattens in London, which had come to the attention of radicals because of its supposed healing powers. The rood was destroyed one night 'by certeine lewde persons, Fleminges and Englishe men'. One of the men was John Gough, a stationer who had previously published reforming books. After the rood breaking there was a serious fire in the parish, incurring several fatalities, which some interpreted as divine vengeance.

The pace of change quickened when Edward VI assumed the throne in 1547. Royal Injunctions issued in 1547 required the destruction of all images of saints, and all images before which candles had been burned. The only lights allowed were on the altar, so candles were now forbidden on the rood loft. Injunctions were enforced by visitations, but there was evidently resistance since by November 1547 the royal visitors were pulling down images in London churches by night. The visitors were allowed discretion with regard to destruction of

Images on the rood screen at Binham Priory were overpainted with texts from the Great Bible on a white background, but over time the images beneath have emerged again. Replacement of the image by the word sums up much of the religious reform of the Reformation.

images, which allowed many images to survive for practical reasons, such as in windows, and perhaps sometimes those painted on screens. Roods were not part of the screen as such and so all of them could be removed. The ultimate success of this policy can be measured by the fact that the survival of medieval roods is very rare. The exceptional rood group in Betws Gwerfil Goch (Denbighshire) was re-assembled as part of a reredos in the 1850s and is still displayed in the church.

One of the more profound changes of Reformation Christianity was the rejection of purgatory and the practices that were dependent upon it. Purgatory, where the sins of the dead are cleansed before they can enter into heaven, is not mentioned in the Bible but became a cornerstone of medieval Christianity. Memorial masses in honour of the dead were a regular feature of medieval worship, and were the reason chantry chapels and guilds were established. When purgatory was declared to be false doctrine, memorial masses became superfluous and by Act of Parliament in 1547 chantries and guilds were closed down. Altars attached to rood screens became redundant and in any case by 1550 all stone altars, with their overtones of sacrifice, were ordered to be removed and replaced with simple wooden communion tables.

Implementation of Edwardian policy varied across the dioceses. Bishop Hooper of Worcester and Gloucester, and Archbishop Cranmer of Canterbury were particularly zealous in the attack on traditional images. Bishop Hooper issued an injunction in 1551 for the removal of rood screens in order that there be no barrier between the minister and his

Defaced images
of the apostles
on the screen
at Marsham
(Norfolk).

people, which is probably why survival of rood screens in Gloucestershire is so poor.

Evidence for the Edwardian destruction of images is visible on many rood screens, on which saints have usually been deliberately damaged by scraping off or scratching out their faces. In churches such as North Burlingham (Norfolk), where the rood screen was made only in 1536, the parishioners who had invested in the visual centrepiece of the parish church must have been mostly still alive to witness the damage that undermined its original purpose. Perhaps some of them had accepted the arguments for reforming the church and joined in. The alternative was to whitewash the dado of the screen, which hid the entire image of the saints. At Binham Priory (Norfolk) the saints were overpainted and texts of the Bible in English were superimposed, symbolising the change in importance from the image to the word in Reformation Christianity. In the process it added another layer of history to the screen. At numerous churches whitewashing preserved the original images, which were not exposed again until the nineteenth century. Some churchwardens' accounts refer to the whitening of the whole church at this time, including the

Defaced images
of saints on
the screen at
Widecombe-
in-the-Moor
(Devon).

walls and the doom painting. Some of these were overpainted
with Biblical texts, like the surviving doom at Wenhaston
(Suffolk). Parclose screens suffered less damage than rood
screens and there were never orders for their removal, although
some of them had images that were defaced.

By the time Edward died in 1553 the colour and visual
splendour of the medieval church was largely gone. Mary
vowed to restore Catholic worship, but changes to the church
had been too profound to make a complete return to what had
gone before. The cost of implementing new policies under her
predecessors, including new books and communion tables,
had strained parish finances and the resources for restoring
traditional religion were therefore limited.

Although the Roman-Catholic liturgy was reintroduced,
memorial masses were never reinstated, so the altars did not
return to the screens. However, Mary appointed conservative
bishops who demanded the restoration of the rood. For
example, in 1555 Bishop Bonner of London ordered his diocese
to re-establish 'a decent and seemly crucifix, with images of
Christ, Mary and John, a roodloft, as in times past hath been

godly used and accustomed of old ancient time'. Bishop Brooks of Gloucester also commanded churchwardens in his diocese to procure a decent rood. Interestingly he stipulated that it should be 'not painted upon cloth or boards, but cut out in timber or stone'. Brooks suggests that impoverished parishes were making do with simple painted images instead of the considerable expense of carved images. One example of a painted rood of Marian date survives in the Norfolk church of Ludham. Parishioners in Morebath (Devon) had taken down and stored parts of the rood loft, which was re-erected in 1554, and perhaps this was common. Elsewhere parishes had to pay to restore what they had previously paid to remove. At Ashburton (Devon) the churchwardens paid 3s 4d for the rood to be taken down in 1548. Then, in Mary's reign, £2 was paid for a new one. In addition the cost of setting it up on the loft was 2d, and 4d was paid for mending the loft, plus 6d to paint over the scriptures painted on the tympanum.

At Ludham (Norfolk) the painted rood set up during the reign of Queen Mary has survived. Many parishes made do with a painted rather than a carved rood when the Catholic liturgy was restored in 1553.

THE CHURCH OF ENGLAND

MARY'S DEATH IN 1558 put an end to the restoration of the traditional ways. Her successor was her half-sister Elizabeth, brought up in the Protestant tradition. Once again the upper echelons of the church were thoroughly purged and a new cohort of bishops appointed. The reforms of Henry VIII and Edward VI were continued, with renewed attacks on imagery and on the rood loft itself. The main purpose of the rood loft was to support the rood and to honour it with lights. If rood lofts were dismantled it would prove harder for the rood to be reinstated in the future and, because of the expense of building them, it would be beyond the means of most parishes to reinstate them. These long-term aims were important while Elizabeth remained unmarried and the future of the Protestant reforms remained precarious. By Royal Order issued in 1561, rood lofts were ordered to be taken down and, if the rood beam itself was to be retained, there should be 'some convenient crest upon the rood beam toward the church'. This would usually have been the Royal Arms, which had been set up in churches ever since Henry VIII became Head of the Church of England.

However, the Order of 1561 specifically stated that there was to 'remain a comely partition betwixt the chancel and the church' and 'that no alteration be otherwise attempted in them'. Churches without screens were ordered to install new ones. In fact the most notable post-Reformation chancel screens belong to the early seventeenth century. A screen

OPPOSITE
The rood screen and loft at Kemsing (Kent) were restored in 1894 and in 1908 Sir Ninian Comper added the rood group.

The chancel screen at Abbey Dore (Herefordshire) was built in the seventeenth century after the former abbey had become a parish church. It has a Royal Arms in place of a rood.

at Rodney Stoke (Somerset) was erected *c.*1625 and is pre-Reformation in character, even incorporating a rood loft. The fine examples at Croscombe (Somerset) and Dore Abbey (Herefordshire, a former monastery converted for parish use) are in contemporary Jacobean style and display the Royal Arms.

Compliance with the order to remove rood lofts seems to have been slow and, probably, reluctant. Reformers remained vehement in their condemnation of rood lofts and diocesan visitations regularly reiterate the need to take down screens well into the 1580s, when attention was diverted to the problem of recusant priests. The parishioners of Stratton (Cornwall) paid for dismantling the loft over a period between 1565 and 1580. The rood loft of Cambridge Great St Mary's was removed in 1562 and, despite being mended in 1566, the whole remaining structure was sold and removed in 1570. Each of these examples shows how dilatory were the parishes in carrying out their instructions. In Devon the policy was enforced with threats of excommunication and was evidently effective – the only surviving loft parapet in the county is at Atherington.

One of the reasons we know that not all lofts and images were removed in the mid-sixteenth century is the Ordinances issued by Parliament in the English Civil War in 1643 and 1644 that prohibited lofts and required the removal of all images. In the east of England the 1643 Ordinance was enforced vigorously on behalf of the Parliamentary authorities by William Dowsing. In his diary he records visiting more than 250 churches in Suffolk and Cambridgeshire, noting the numbers of 'superstitious pictures' that he had destroyed, some of which must have been on rood screens (many of the others were stained glass).

Antiquarian interest in medieval works of art began in the eighteenth century. However, in this period the screen was often regarded as visually intrusive and many were reduced or removed altogether. In a ten year period between 1727 and 1737 seventy-one medieval rood screens were taken down in Yorkshire alone. A less drastic alternative was to take the screen down to dado level.

When screens were taken down parts could be re-used for pews, pulpits, tower screens and west galleries, which is how many fine medieval works have survived. The trend towards removal of rood screens continued into the nineteenth century. Even in the century that brought us the Gothic Revival the record

Veranda posts and the loft front of the medieval rood screen were re-used to create this west gallery at Strensham (Worcestershire), with saints repainted in the nineteenth century.

Sir George Gilbert Scott restored the church at Adderbury (Oxfordshire) in the 1860s and reinstated this rood loft.

of architects and parishes with regard to medieval rood screens is mixed. A.W.N. Pugin (1812–52), an influential voice in the nineteenth-century Gothic Revival, criticised the destruction of rood screens, which was continuing at a time when they were gaining prestige as valuable works of English medieval Christianity. Many Gothic-Revival architects chose to remove medieval screens, preferring an 'authentic' fourteenth-century

The rood screen dominates the interior of Llangwm Uchaf (Monmouthshire), but it is mainly a sensitive reconstruction in the 1870s by the architect J.P. Seddon.

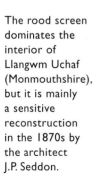

appearance. Screens interrupted a view of the east window, which became the visual focus of the interior. Architects also liked to raise the level of the chancel by means of steps, in which context the presence of a screen was visually wrong and awkward in practice. Removal of screens continued beyond the late nineteenth century. A survey made in 1886 recorded 119 rood screens in Norfolk with figure paintings, but in the subsequent century and quarter twenty-one of those screens have been completely removed.

Loss of screens coincided with a period when other rood screens were restored to their original glory. Some Victorian architects, like Sir George Gilbert Scott (1811–1878), were generally in favour of screens, but most restoration of screens was the work of the next generation of architects, beginning in the final quarter of the nineteenth century. Harry Hems (1842–1916) and Herbert Read (1860–1904) were responsible for the restoration of many screens in Devon from the 1870s to the Edwardian period. In the process some fragile medieval paintings were cleaned (and sometimes over-cleaned) and many have been repainted. Repainting has also covered the muntins, tracery, coving and bressumers of rood screens, restoring the original brightly coloured appearance, although the modern taste often prefers the grain and tone of the aged wood. There have also been many significant discoveries. The fine painted dado panels at Ipplepen (Devon) were revealed by Herbert Read during restoration in 1898 when a layer of brown paint was removed.

Although the restoration of screens in the nineteenth century belongs to a pre-conservation era, the early restorers did valuable work in making records of the screens as they existed then. Professor E.W. Tristram made drawings of screens in Norfolk and Suffolk. David Walker, architect of Llananno church in the

The twentieth-century rood screen at Kettlebaston (Suffolk) was designed by the incumbent, Father Ernest Geldart, and painted in 1949 by Patrick Osborne, with figures added in 1954 by Enid Chadwick. It is a monument to the high-church Anglo-Catholicism of the early twentieth century.

Sir Ninian Comper's screen at Lound (Suffolk) was erected on the eve of the First World War and includes an altar dedicated to Our Lady that was inspired by the medieval screen at Ranworth.

1870s, made a detailed drawing of the rood screen before the church was rebuilt. The careful restoration of screens has been in the hands of professional conservators from the 1960s, with leading lights Pauline Plummer in East Anglia and Anna Hulbert in Devon.

Some Gothic-Revival architects were interested in church furnishings and new screens often became part of their design. Unlike the medieval period, the screen now came within the brief of the architect. New screens were often built because they made a physical separation between the nave and chancel, heightening the sanctity and mystery of the east end of the church in a period when the sacraments had been re-established as the most important element of Christian worship. The Church of England was a broad Church, and its Anglo-Catholic adherents continued to build rood screens in parish churches until the mid-twentieth century. Church furnishings became an important part of the architectural practice of Sir Ninian Comper (1864–1960), who is the architect most closely associated with the revival of screenwork and the Anglo-Catholic enrichment of church interiors. He restored and constructed new rood screens in a variety of churches, the aim of which was partly to fulfil the church's practical needs, but also to celebrate the English architectural and ecclesiastical character. This was best demonstrated by the interior of his own church at Wellingborough St Mary, where the painted chancel screen is replete with painted and relief figures, but much of his work on rood screens was carried out in medieval churches. Other architects were doing the same, restoring roods (not always with historical accuracy) to old rood lofts and adding them to new ones. In doing so they have acknowledged the central place of rood screens in our religious and cultural heritage.

FURTHER READING

Details of rood screens can be found in the volumes of *The Buildings of England* and *The Buildings of Wales* by Sir Nikolaus Pevsner and others, which indicate which churches have rood screens worth visiting. Some parts of England are also well served by online church guides, which are listed below. There have been surprisingly few publications devoted to screens, but the most relevant are:

Baker, Audrey. *English Panel Paintings 1400–1558: A Survey of Figure Paintings on East Anglian Rood Screens.* Archetype Publications (2011)

Vallance, Aymer. *English Church Screens: Being Great Roods, Screenwork and Rood-lofts of Parish Churches in England and Wales.* Batsford (1936; long out of print but still available second-hand)

Wheeler, Richard. *The Medieval Church Screens of the Southern Marches.* Logaston Press (2006)

ONLINE SOURCES

www.kentchurches.info
www.norfolkchurches.co.uk/mainpage.htm
www.suffolkchurches.co.uk/churchlists.htm

PLACES TO VISIT

The distribution of surviving rood screens in England and Wales is very uneven, with few survivals in the north of England. For quantity and quality Devon, Norfolk and, to a lesser extent, Suffolk, are outstanding, and painted screen images are largely confined to these counties. The bar for selection is set higher here than for other counties. Chancel screens which are wholly of the post-Reformation period are marked with *. A painted rood screen in a recreated church interior of c.1530 can be seen in St Teilo's church at St Fagans, National Museum of History, near Cardiff.

ENGLAND
BEDFORDSHIRE: Marston Moretaine, Oakley*
BERKSHIRE: Warfield
BUCKINGHAMSHIRE: Edlesborough, North Crawley, Wing
CHESHIRE: Astbury, Daresbury, Mobberley
CORNWALL: Blisland*, Lanreath, Little Petherick*, St Buryan, St Ewe, St Levan, St Winnow, Sancreed
DERBYSHIRE: Kirk Langley
DEVON: Alphington (Exeter), Ashton, Atherington, Awliscombe, Berry Pomeroy, Blackawton, Bovey Tracey, Bradninch, Bridford, Broadhempston, Buckland-in-the-moor, Burrington, Cheriton Bishop, Chawleigh, Chivelstone, Chudleigh, Chumleigh, Coldridge, Colebrooke, Colyton, Dartmouth St Saviour, Dunchideok, East Allington, East Portlemouth, Feniton, Halberton, Harberton, Hartland, Holbeton, Ipplepen, Kenn, Kentisbeare, Kenton, Kings Nympton, Lapford, Lustleigh, Manaton, Marwood, Morchard Bishop, Nymet Tracey, Paignton St John*, Parracombe, Payhembury, Pilton, Pinhoe (Exeter), Plymtree, Sherford, South Pool, Staverton, Stokeinteignhead, Swimbridge, Talaton, Tawstock, Torbryan, Totnes

St Mary, Uffculme, Ugborough, Welcombe,
Widecombe-in-the-moor, Willand
DORSET: Bradford Abbas, Cerne Abbas, Folke*, Trent,
Wimborne St Giles*
ESSEX: Castle Hedingham, Corringham, Finchingfield,
Great Bardfield, Henham, Manuden, Stebbing
GLOUCESTERSHIRE: Ashchurch, Berkeley
HAMPSHIRE: Basingstoke, Bramley, Chilbolton,
Dummer, Hurstbourne Tarrant, Silchester, Winchester
St John the Baptist
HEREFORDSHIRE: Aymestrey, Burghill, Eyton,
Llandinabo, Michaelchurch, St Margarets, Welsh Newton
HERTFORDSHIRE: Baldock, King's Walden
KENT: Brenchley, Capel-le-Ferne St Mary, Eastchurch,
Higham, Kemsing, Leeds, Lullingstone, Northfleet,
Shoreham, Westwell
LANCASHIRE: Huyton, Manchester Cathedral,
Middleton, Northenden (Manchester), Sefton
LEICESTERSHIRE: Long Whatton
LINCOLNSHIRE: Coates-by-Stow,
Huttoft, Theddlethorpe
LONDON: St Cyprian Clarence Gate*,
St Paul's Knightsbridge*
NORFOLK: Acle, Attleborough, Aylsham, Barton Turf,
Binham Priory, Brettenham, Castle Acre, Catfield, Cawston,
Dersingham, East Harling, Edgefield, Edingthorpe,
Emneth, Fakenham, Filby, Fritton, Fundenhall, Gateley,
Great Snoring, Happisburgh, Hempstead, Horsford,
Horsham St Faith, Litcham, Ludham, Loddon, Marsham,
North Burlingham, North Walsham, Ranworth,
Sheringham, South Walsham, Sparham, Swanton Abbot,
Thompson, Tunstead, Worstead, Yelverton
NORTHAMPTONSHIRE: Ashby St Ledgers, Bozeat,
Braybrooke, Geddington, Wellingborough All Hallows,
Wellingborough St Mary*

ABOVE LEFT
The deep and re-painted coving of the late-medieval screen at Charlton-on-Otmoor (Oxfordshire).

ABOVE RIGHT
Intricate tracery is carved into the dado of the rood screen at Hughley (Shropshire).

Many medieval rood screens have been repainted to reproduce their original bright colours, like this example at Long Sutton (Somerset).

NOTTINGHAMSHIRE: Egmanton
OXFORDSHIRE: Adderbury, Barford St Michael, Bloxham, Brize Norton, Charlton-on-Otmoor, Church Hanborough, Deddington, Ewelme, Great Rollright, Somerton, Stanton St John, Stanton Harcourt
SHROPSHIRE: Hughley, Lydbury North
SOMERSET: Banwell, Bishops Lydeard, Brushford, Carhampton, Croscombe*, Culbone, Dunster, Halse,

Long Ashton, Long Sutton, Low Ham*, Minehead,
Queen Camel, Rodney Stoke*, Trull, Watchet
STAFFORDSHIRE: Clifton Campville, Swynnerton
SUFFOLK: Barking, Bedfield, Bramfield, Bramford,
Dennington, Denston, Elmswell*, Eye, Grundisburgh,
Hitcham, Kedington, Kettlebaston*, Lavenham, Lound*,
Risby, Somerleyton, Southwold, Westhall, Woolpit,
Wyverstone, Yaxley
SURREY: Charlwood, Gatton
WARWICKSHIRE: Alcester, Knowle,
Merevale, Wormleighton
WILTSHIRE: Avebury, Compton Bassett, Mere, Salisbury
Sarum St Martin
WORCESTERSHIRE: Besford, Little Malvern, Shelsley
Walsh, Strensham
YORKSHIRE: Aysgarth, Cantley*, Flamborough,
Hubberholme, Leeds St John*, Skipton

WALES

ANGLESEY: Llaneilian
CONWY: Conwy, Llanrwst
DENBIGHSHIRE: Betws Gwerfil Goch, Clocaenog,
Derwen, Llanelidan, Llanrhydd
GWYNEDD: Clynnog Fawr, Llanengan
MERIONETH: Llanegryn
MONMOUTHSHIRE:
Bettws Newydd,
Llangwm Uchaf, Usk
POWYS: Beguildy, Cascob,
Cregrina, Llananno,
Llandefalle, Llanelieu,
Llanfilo, Llanwnnog,
Old Radnor, Partrishow,
Pennant Melangell
WREXHAM: Gresford

Original stencilled paintwork survives on the coving of the rood screen at Beguildy (Powys).

INDEX

Page numbers in bold refer to illustrations

Abbey Dore 54, **54**
Acle **31**
Adderbury **56**
Alblastyr, John and Benedicta 17
Albrede, John and Agnes 17
Alphington 36
Ashburton 51
Ashton 37, **37**
Atherington **20**
Attleborough **7**, 26
Aylsham **17**
Aymestrey **25**

Banwell 19
Barking **13**
Barfreston 10
Barton Turf 34, **34**
Baymont, John 18, **18**
Beguildy **63**
Bell, Roger 18
Bennet, Thomas 17–18
Bettws Newydd **26**
Betws Gwerfil Goch 48
Binham Priory **48**, 49
Binstead 26
Blackawton 30, **44**
Blake, John and Cecily 17–18
Bletchingley 45
Bodmin 17
Bonner, Bishop Edmund 50–1
Bonversall, Michael 18, 21
Bovey Tracey **16**, 34
Boxley 46–7
Bradford-on-Avon 9, 12
Bramfield **33**
Brenchley 45
Bridford **38**
Bristol
  All Saints 32
  St Ewens 40
Brixworth 9
Brooks, Bishop James 51
Broughton **24**
Brushford 18, **19**
Burghill 24

Cambridge, St Mary the Great 18, 54
Campeggio, Lorenzo 47
Canterbury
  Holy Cross 18
  St Pancras 9
Cawston **30**, 36

Chadwick, Enid **57**
Charlton-on-Otmoor **62**
Chawleigh 21
Chester, Alice 32
Chilham 40
Chittlehampton 35
Chudleigh **33**, 34
Church Hanborough **41**
Clayton 12–13
Clemens, Richard 17
Comper, Sir Ninian **52**, 58, **58**
Coombs 12–13
Coventry, Holy Trinity 27
Cranbrook 45
Cranmer, Archbishop Thomas 48
Creche, John 21
Crediton 10
Croscombe 54
Crosse, John 21
Cullompton 26–7

Daw, John 20, 21
Doom painting 27, **27**, 50
Dovercourt 46
Dowsing, William 55
Dunster **11**

Easton-in-Gordano 18
Edingthorpe **12**
Escomb 9
Eton College 19
Exeter, St Petroc 39

Foxe, John 46
Foxley 18, **18**

Gateley 36
Gazeley 18
Geldart, Ernest **57**
Glastonbury, St John the Baptist 12, 16
Grantham 40
Great Bardfield **8**, 23

Hackington 18, 21
Headbourne Worthy 12
Hems, Harry 57
Hennock **31**, **35**, 36, 37
Henry VIII, King 47
Honiton 17, 40
Hooper, Bishop John 48–9
Horsham St Faith 32, **32**
Hughley **62**
Hulbert, Anna 58

Ipplepen 35, **36**, 57
Ipswich, St Matthew 16–17

Kemsing **52**
Kentisbeare **16**, 29
Kenton 34
Kettlebaston **57**
Kings Nympton **27**
Kirkstead 9

Lanfranc, Archbishop 12
Litcham 36–7
Llananno 5, **6**, 26, 57–8
Llandefalle 5, 26, **26**
Llanegryn 5
Llanelieu 5, 24, **25**
Llangwm Uchaf **56**
Loddon 37, **37**
London 10
  St Margaret Pattens 47
  St Thomas of Acre 19
Long Sutton **62**
Lound **58**
Louth 40
Ludham 51, **51**
Ludlow 40

Malmesbury Abbey 40
Marsham **49**
Martin, Thomas 39
Martyn, Roger 42–3
Marwood 30
Morebath 18, 21, 51
Mottes, John 15

North Burlingham 17–18, **46**, 49
North Elmham 36, **36**
Nun, John 18
Nymet Tracey **14**

Old Shoreham 26
Osborne, Patrick **57**
Ottery St Mary 10

Painter, John 21
Parclose screen 12, **13**, 50
Pares, John 20, 21
Partrishow 5, **22**, 43, **43**
Patcham 27
Pennant Melangell 26
Pilton 39
Pixley 11
Plummer, Pauline 58
Plymtree **4**, 37
Popyll, William 18, 21
Pugin, A.W.N. 56
Pulpitum 9–10

Ranworth 34, **42**, 43
Read, Herbert 57
Reculver 9
Repton 9

Rickmansworth 45–6
Ringland **47**
Rivenhall 11
Rochester Cathedral 9
Rodney Stoke 54
Roods 12, 26, 27, 39–40, 41, 45–8, 50–1
Royal Arms 54, **54**

St Columb Major 20
St Kew 20
St Levan 30
St Margarets **13**, 24
Salisbury, St Thomas 27
Schorne, Sir John **35**, 36
Scott, Sir George Gilbert **56**, 57
Sedding, E.H. 20
Seddon, J.P. **56**
South Pool 30
Southwold 17, 34
Stanton Harcourt 9, **10**
Stebbing 23
Stratton 19–21, 31, 54
Strensham **55**
Suffield 36

Tackle, Joan 17
Thompson 30
Thorpe by Haddiscoe 15
Tintinhull 12
Torbryan **28**, 32, 37
Triplow 18
Tristram, E.W. 57
Trunch 15

Walker, David 57–8
Week St Mary 20
Wellingborough, St Mary 58
Wellingham **42**
Welsh Newton **11**
Wenhaston 27, **27**, 50
West Harnham 11
Westhall 36
Westwell 39
Whimple **35**
Widecombe-in-the-Moor **50**
Willingham 30
Winchester College 19
Wolborough 35, 36
Woodbridge 17
Worstead 17
Wulcy, William 32
Wymer, Thomas **17**

Yatton 12, 18, 21